Dante's Heaven

Jan Kemp

Auckland
Puriri Press 2006

ISBN 0-908943-30-x

Acknowledgements
Many of these poems first appeared in other publications and on-line, so thanks are due to the editors of: *Ariel, brief, JAAM, Landfall, NZ Books, nzepc, NZ Listener, Poetry NZ, Trout, Turbine* & *WLWE* (now the *Journal of Post-Colonial Writing*).

creative nz
ARTS COUNCIL OF NEW ZEALAND *TOI AOTEAROA*

Grateful thanks to Creative New Zealand
for a writer's grant to complete this collection

By the same author

Poetry

Only One Angel University of Otago Press, Dunedin, 2001
The Sky's Enormous Jug Puriri Press, Auckland, 2001
The Other Hemisphere Three Continents Press, Washington DC; Butterfly Books, NSW , 1991
Five Poems, Arte & Materia, Singapore, (pamphlet) 1988
Ice-Breaker Poems, Coal-Black Press, Auckland, (pamphlet) 1980
Diamonds & Gravel Hampson Hunt, Wellington, 1979
Against the Softness of Woman Caveman Press, Dunedin, 1976

Editorial

Aotearoa New Zealand Poetry Sound Archive Founding director (co-director Jack Ross), 2004
NZ Poets Read Their Work & New Zealand Poets Read their Work for Children, a 3LP set
Founding co-collector & co-editor (with Jonathan Lamb & Alan Smythe), Waiata Recordings Archive, 1974

to Dieter
who said
be all the voices

contents

dante's heaven

10 Crux Australis — Te Paki o Autahi — Southern Cross
11 Lily
12 Dante's 'heaven'
13 'We are all newcomers'
16 Apparitions of angels
17 Sailing boats
18 Our paradise
19 Naked ladies near Otama Beach, Coromandel Peninsula
20 The past present/s
22 A pukeko's trip south
24 Swimming

tributes

26 Eloquence
27 A stand of cannas
28 Bowl spoon table
29 Ming-blue fish
30 Down to the ground
31 Best friends
32 A childhood secret
33 A poet on two crescents
36 Glance

requiems

38 On news of a poet's death
42 Watching Eileen at a poet's wake
43 Nikau at Punakaiki
44 Requiem at Torbay
45 Staunch
47 Silence / speech
48 Turning

love is a babe

a sequence of poems mostly around Beatrice's voice . . .

50 Love is a babe
51 A portrait of Dante's younger self
52 Someone kissed me
53 E la selva oscura, non cè?
54 Mercury
55 The pure white diamond Dante brought to Beatrice
56 He reads his poem aloud
57 Beatrice denies Dante her greeting . . .
58 Being Beatrice
59 Jousting
60 Meeting up with Dante down under
61 Beatus

notes

62

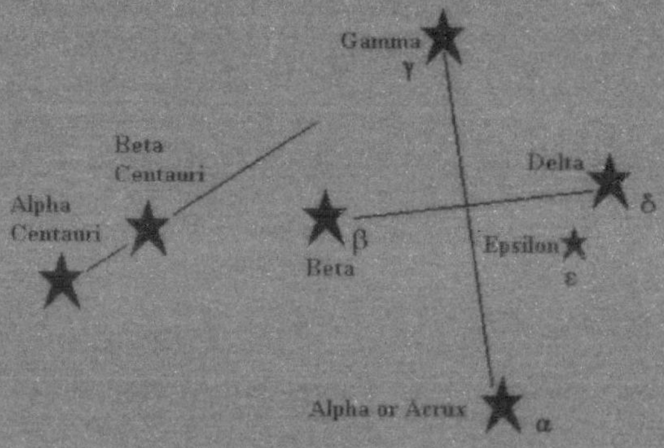
Gamma
γ
Beta
Centauri
Alpha
Centauri
Delta
δ
β
Beta
Epsilon
ε
Alpha or Acrux
α

dante's 'heaven'

'To get back up to the shining world from there
My guide and I went into that hidden tunnel:

And following its path, we took no care
To rest, but climbed: he first, then I—so far,
Through a round aperture I saw appear

Some of the beautiful things that Heaven bears,
Where we came forth, and once more saw the stars.'

— *Dante Alighieri*

Crux Australis—
Te Paki o Autahi—
Southern Cross

'I turned to the right and considered the other pole,
and I saw four stars never seen except by the first people.'

He never saw this kite of four stars
yet knew they existed—heart map of home, our palm, hemisphere
where we know where we are upside down near the pole.

Somehow he knew Eden is here
& we hand on the sunrise
from Mt Hikurangi, a flaming canna.

And Dante, pilgrim, could have climbed up
out of the shaft, plumb opposite Jerusalem, to stand
ankle-deep in the Pacific, on a shoal near the Kermadecs

awestruck at seeing his cardinal virtues
incarnate, white, on the milk near Centaurus—
Justice, Prudence, Temperance & Fortitude,
rocks the gods had flung out of the back yard,
making space to plant the herbs
of faith, hope and aroha.

Lily

Dante, be in the lily's scroll
become calligraphy of sound & sight
in this green space

this place you name Purgatorio—
which though not paradise
we call heaven.

Dante's 'heaven'

We two fallen through earth's core
beached here at Mt Purgatory
blink back antipodean light
days on end.

There's sky enough to dive into
islands in green-blue water
to swim to.

Heaven to be earthly
looking up nightly
at the blackness
milky with stars.

‘We are all newcomers’

to Allen Curnow & Hone Tuwhare

I

Who came first is indisputable—
accretions & cooling in space in place in time
to make her—
vapours liquefying into oceans
where primal movers of the vegetable/animal kingdoms
precurse in Darwinian Ur-language
the stuttering of all our tribes—great vowel shifts
across continents, somnambulant as oxen, fires burning behind
we shambled across earth’s face
she we love without thought—terra firma   papa tuanuku—
since we stood (trying not to walk on her orifices)
she took us in
from our wet sunset-drenched sunrise endless
blue period on the saturating Medusa raft sea
she said *Land Ahoy, boy!* to Kupe, to Nick—
she stretched her shore
and lay before—
‘we are all newcomers’.

II

To build the nest of his octet
Mendelssohn took two quartets of strings
took skittering tripping feet alighting on sound
took the flurry of gathered twigs
all rubbed up into heat.

III

On toe point, taiaha balanced,
tongue challenging his chin,
a warrior foots it forward
to lay a welcome bone-blade, fern or feather,
we are here now together—
whatever notes pierced the silence at our births,
whatever tribe they, whatever Maori we
despatched with mere & execution of treaty.

IV

On Long Bay beach the languages
of sky of sea of land, and of the newest
comers speaking Samoan, Croatian
Hindi, Italian, Afrikaans, Arabic, Mandarin
overheard in just one swim
from three to seven pines and back—
in a half hour Maori and English
made plankton shoaling through
the incoming whale tide of costumes and custom—
of covering uncovering corpus delectum,
do you or don't you show in Aotearoa?

V

Speak the words on your tongue—
'the poets are the soul of a country'.

Hone, the words change, are changing!

Snatch & make them yours, woman—
take a stick, scrawl in sand, catch
air-castles, watch, listen, see, hear:
our task is speech, getting it all down
still plenty of breathing room
and Ruaumoko snorting underfoot.

Apparitions of angels

after the Italian Trecento

Flocks of white caps near The Noises—
overhead a bi-plane (could be Saint-Exupéry)
& Icarus, sky-diving from the cliff:

these winged things on powder-blue
you'd think you'd walked into a Giotto
or sun-struck with gold a Cimabue—

& you, 'like a Virgin'.

Sailing boats

Watch from the deck
the origami Ps
& optimist Qs
slip off
the tide's tongue

bob out
into the bay—
wayang kulit
gone to sea

white napkins
nodding together
on a pulled
turquoise cloth.

Our paradise

Rangi's rainbow
isolates
on Papa
a succulent fern

shaping

Tane's koru
into a tui's
white-tufted
teardrop of song.

Naked ladies near Otama Beach, Coromandel Peninsula

L. *Amaryllis* f. Gk *Amarullus,* a country girl in Theocritis, Virgil and Ovid. A bulbous plant of the genus *Amaryllis,* or formerly of this genus, which now contains only one species (the southern African *A. belladonna,* belladonna lily).

Partying at paddock edges, undressed on wine-red stalks
they flaunt ripped bodices, shake back pink hair

laughing at the solemnity of steers spending the day
grazing up a hill's rump to become a skyline caravanserai

you could pinprick into Taurus Minor or Major
once the night sky pulls down the drop of galaxies without end—

opera in the park   free entrance   and bums-on-seats the beach
as the steer bellows his horns out and the chorus twirls.

The sea's the best of orchestras—as the last fling of foam hiss-whispers
back another breaker bashes down 'as clear as God or glass'

and you the audience are in the swim. And that plasmic sea
cannot beat or break without the *Bang & Olufsen* of your heart.

The past present/s

'I am very desirous of seeing the good Lady's face, as she now appears, with old age creeping up on her. I should chuse her painted on a small half length . . . sitting in as natural a posture as possible. I shall leave the picturesque disposition intirely to yourself and I shall only observe that gravity is the choice of Dress.'

John Greenwood in London to John Singleton Copley in Boston, Spring 1770

Mrs Humphrey Devereux in Te Papa—
a full octave of generations removed,
present in a gilt frame, sitting upright
at a Pembroke table, left arm gloved
in black from elbow to half-hand,
she rests the sapphire-ringed
forefinger on the others on the long
winkingly-polished mahogany.

Her right hand & forearm bare,
forefinger on one cheek, her chin
rests there in the easy groove between
thumb and folded second finger—her
crisply bonneted face quite manly
about the nose and brow. Her grey-blue
eyes look simultaneously steady into
all worlds—present, past and future.

At 70 in Autumn 1770, she sat for it—
three husbands behind her. Son of her first,
Samuel Greenwood, John the painter's
second son, (also) John's son, our
John Danforth Greenwood came with
Sarah Field, his wife, five children and
The Portrait of Mrs Humphrey Devereux
on board the *Phoebe* in 1853, to Motueka;

& now, counting down the branches
of their tree: John Graham Mary,
Ellen Jane Charles, Agnes Alfred Frederick,
Annie Fanny Charlotte (who married
Dr William Kemp, my grandfather's father)
and not to forget their thirteenth Katy,
there is me. So he'd know how his mother
looked in age—after the death of his father,

re-married to a Mr Prince who died, re-married
to H.D. & she long gone to America—John
(the painter) commissioned *Mrs H.D.* from
his friend Delacroix's friend, the Bostonian
John Singleton Copley (who did the first racy
portrait of a lady, Turkish fashion in a turban,
Mrs Thomas Gage (Margaret Kemble), 'the Duchess',
'he made her a sultana' in New York,

her head 'full of untold thoughts',
her white elbow sinking into a cushion.
Our four times great grandmother
sits in keeping with ideal, polite posture.
She has solemnity—a beauty becoming her age
eclipsing raciness and her own gravely fine clothes—
There's a clear calm in her face
& I think how much she's seen, this

Miss Mary Charnock of Yorkshire,
London & Boston, painted in her
seventieth year, now permanent resident
here. I whisper to her how good it is
being so many times so greatly related (in
grand-daughterly fashion) to a portrait.

A pukeko's trip south

Northern swamp hen
with red sticky beak
stilt legs bright blue breast
& beady eye spies—

at Tekapo   a chapel   stones
a glacial lake   the palest opaque
turquoise & the air knife-biting clear.
Roadside berries fur-brown

sideways-folding hills—
Pukaki's lake a peacock blue
fanning into shingled feathers
rivulets of glaciers.

From sun-broken boulders
look & look at Hooker Lake
icebergs   white-grey water
and up & up at staggering

back Aoraki / Mt Cook.
Down & over two swing bridges
glimpses of the cliff behind
the tussock grass the flax beneath

don't look now but quickly
snatch the riverbed   the Hooker's
rush, at every step when looking up
Mt Sefton nodding under snow.

Being south I don't much miss
my mangrove isthmus harbours
insects crawling on warmed mud
shawls of squalling showers.

Not very migratory
yet happy to holiday
pecking my way along—
pukeko pukeko.

Swimming

Nothing reduces you to your skin like the sea—cold
plunge into reality, a tongue already salty & all that power
self-propelling you through our other element

body loving every pummelling second as your mind slips
on the (no wonder) Madonna-blue beach wrap of the sky.
The straightest line imaginable just over the breakers

visibly separating the two, doesn't exist.
You do. Yet, can you hold a handful of salt water
to prove it for just one moment before you go.

tributes

Eloquence

to Ian Wedde

Great to be back inside your head that hour you read
busking your way into ours Horace basking alongside

the boom lowered to the commonplace &
that sail your bursting heart lifting up Mt Victoria—

a glorious day one out of the box golden boy of the sixties
at 55 balding black-suited still maybe shouting *fuck* inside

but no longer needing to behave badly, talking friends/fathering/
storms of taste cooked up in the kitchen/your Gemini twin brother

& your own father's fading into the pale Agfa horizon
of his coloured slides from six tin trunks—how I remember

your mother on the Karnifuli river boat tossing the piss
overboard—how what matters is not to waste a minute.

Hearing you is a swim in what you name for us so lightly
the mirror you've held up to lieutenant life who looks

back at you getting wiser sadder, the reviewers say, getting truer—
it's humbling, the man sitting next to me remarks, *to hear you*

the pick of our generation—lush ebullient intellectual bullshit-
artist of the first water, still making waves where our hearts beach

hauling in your net to pick through the days of where we've been
and might be. The banal but lifted. Paradise yes, 'but earthly'.

It's good you say it's shaky sand you prefer
to stand on. It throws the view right out.

A stand of cannas

to Nicki

Turbans & trumpets flaming a gully's hillside—
you'd think they're from India or Pakistan
spelt like Khandallah and the Khyber Pass

& in winter, foot soldiers
under swaddling felt
waiting for summer to flare

but cannas come from tropical America
& blare their crushed flames
in riot everywhere.

Bowl spoon table

to Michael Smither

That grey bowl you painted
with its rim shadowed

& that spoon with its shadow
on that wooden table

& in its shadow the filled softer-grey hypotenuse
from the floor up to it—

how big everything was
so much bigger

than us doing the looking

& how full of nothing

but spaces

round the painted shapes.

Ming-blue fish

to Michael Smither

Ming-blue fish through polyps of pink coral
swim in and out of your brain (that head

of cauliflower you wouldn't be without
within yourself & despite white butterflies).

Snorkelling along, flipping fins, thinking of nothing
a movement to adjust your mask

& the fish dart, are gone & reappear
sensing a clear coast, white shelled sand

a lagoon to eddy around, day-dream in, with a
a rock to cling to, when surf dashes the slope

breakers furling. On the cliff a dog frets
by the four wheel drive for two wet-suited riders

to loom back up the beach. You 'look,
look well'. See clear enough to paint.

Down to the ground

to Riemke Ensing
on her birthday, 24 May 2004

Everything suits, when you think of it:
there's just the right phrasing
or there's a pause—music, of course, or
a poem—that goes without saying

as when the evening falls over the sea
& on the blank flat surface of quietened water
a fisherman dips the oars & you happen to notice
walking the shore jumping the rivulets
to the firm sand of Deep Creek run out to sea,
where the palest of blues this side of the city,
round the double-coned bush-covered island
fades into pink, as your eye lifts from dinghy to sky:

back home you walk, briskly, it's a quarter to six
& you're astonished night has already fallen
right down to the ground moving under your feet.

Best friends

to Morrin Madill Rout

Their mothers, Wendy and Joan, 'd be so thrilled if they'd known
their daughters 'd meet now, both 51 with reddened hair and plump

as the baby cheeks they knew better than them, one out one in
the door of Hamilton's maternity ward the same year.

Best friends smiling in hats & gloves carrying christened
babies in the boom time—Waikato fathers out of uniform

at the show grounds for Jackson's herds, Morice's cars.
In the Diocesan School for Girls' cubicle, a silver mirror

& hairbrush Wendy gave her boarding-school Rapunzel; on Joan's
daughter's wrist, the snake bangle she never quite understood

from godmother—were Joan to die she'd belong to Peter Pan & come,
an orphan, to live in Wendy's tree-house to grow up. She'd have a sister.

They'll meet, Wendy's daughter with daughter, Joan's without,
see how they've spent their mothers' legacy since childhood

one dead, one without memory, fairies now, both lost and found.

A childhood secret

They were the first lovers I ever knew of
held in a house behind a paddock of daffodils
& I mustn't tell.

Wife-less, lifelong he loved her
& I'd see her empty car parked under trees—
tartan rug & picnic basket from the back seat, gone.

They'd go in his car
to places he'd chosen in the bush, by a waterfall,
places less open

than his metal road where she first stopped
when he waved
& came from the cow-shed to talk to her

his eyes cupped against the light
& with a hand more electric than a fence
touched her sun-browned arm.

One son, a cerebral husband and now he,
who held her fifty years
all gone—& she at eighty-one,

my other mother, here.
How he still holds her & the yellow flowers
she stands cradling.

A poet on two crescents

'Writing is learning how to die' — Ilse Eichinger

I — Two 'high priests' on Tohunga Crescent

Purely accidental the addresses were similar
only the street numbers differed
and the minds of the men
and what they said
under the red pohutukawa
umbrellaed across the macadam
two Antipodean sons puppeteering
two whip-cracking ring-masters
of two particular circuses
each true to his own
it couldn't be other
I hear the older wise-one whisper
his dog bouncing around his feet

two talking on one crescent
collecting the TLS or LRB from one or other letterbox
chewing over words in the middle of the road
high priests of criticism & poetry
incandescing metaphor's fire
from the rubbed sticks of thought
the poetry out of the poet out of the time
where light sound sight presence
memory vocabulary the flights of a well-read mind
'schreiben ist sterben lernen'
we go as we come
coalesce.

II — A crescent

If it were a matter of belief
or the other for that matter, if it matters at all he piped (up) again
he'd know a way to approach it
you hadn't yet thought of
till gladdened by knowing it seemed you owned such thoughts—
your spinning head a prayer wheel
something never-to-be-forgotten magnified ever after
read once in a Tibetan book
look let's face it he wouldn't have been caught dead reading
but appeared to you to know purely instinctively
his imperturbability a means of shielding diffidence finding
a voice on the wing
that is for each your own & actual
in the bottom of a throat
something you might look for
a lost pen perhaps—

oh, there it is!
slipped into the sofa's seam
while the mind continues to map
the actual matters at stake
seeing a way through its own porticos—
and we discover after all he meant what he said.

III — One poet on another crescent

A poet falls off logs writing poems
or walks along a sewer pipe when the tide's out
watching herons crest ashore
over the mudflats
not putting a foot wrong
but one before the other
on the horizontal
and without looking down
an acrobat
born with a good score
he earned his mangrove stick with which to tap the floor.

Anybody home? over by the green boatsheds
booming down into the belly of the earth—
reflected up above from the shining mud
himself balanced on the far end of a sickle—
a geyser of laughter rips back, *Yeah us,*
Papatuanuku and Hine-nui-te-po, you old tohunga waiata.

Glance

to Anna Wirz-Justice

By the time we are old
we shall know one another
with a glance

as the gods would
had they cared
for friendship.

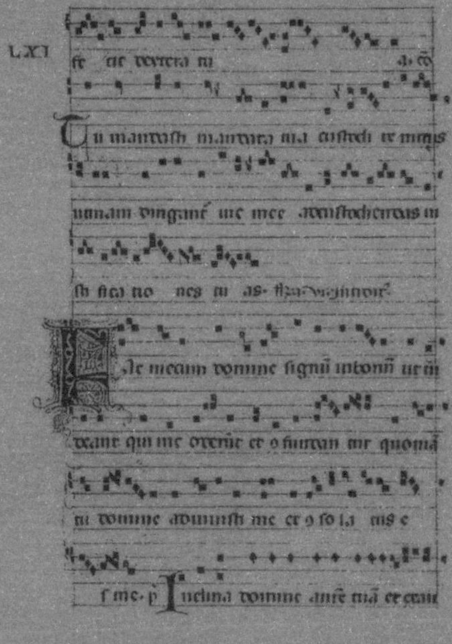
LXI
Tu mandasti mandata tua custodiri nimis
utinam dirigantur vie mee ad custodiendas iu
stificationes tuas.
Fac mecum domine signum in bonum ut vi
deant qui me oderunt et confundantur quoniam
tu domine adiuvisti me et consolatus es
me.
Inclina domine aurem tuam et exaudi

requiems

On news of a poet's death

i.m. Allen Curnow 1911–2001

a cycle of poems for Jeny Curnow

I A hard act to follow

The wind's been kicking his apple-box
all night all day up this steep autumn-strewn street
and it won't be knocked down—
for nothing flattens things built to last.

Men and women make museums to glass in
old Venuses, fractured skulls
a near complete necklace of human teeth
a grave of prehistoric horses housing the past
to know where our stand starts
and how long will Art last?

Buddhas knocked out of recognition
what he still would have written
I so wanted to know.

His apple box kicks on
bovver-booted by a wind by which
he always saw sharply enough to clock a direction
nor' nor' east nor' west or north or south
depending where he stood
and it was here—
where we must pick up the traces.

II Lone kauri wildling

Under a clouded northern moon
I see the kauri he went round
the back of the bach to find for us

pure bach like Bach
not a note missed
teardrop of a tui
scallop shell for a butter dish
coat on a coat-peg
music cobwebbing
up through bush-green
catching the sunlight
spilled silver paint
cathedral pillars

a tree that grows straight up to the light.

A kauri doesn't like to be alone.
We planted it close to other things—a stump
of pohutukawa spouting a David Tua topknot
some wannabe orchids lavender self-seeded pansies.
It's a wildling.
Like foundling?
Yes. A new word for you?

III Der Grimming

We worked it out later—
as he died we'd walked
in the Austrian countryside.

The path through wet birch trees
behind the museum of Heimat treasures
in the chateau at Trautenfels
led past a cowshed, apple trees, fields.

We turned and saw Der Grimming
big grey mountain brimming
the tops of the clouds
its granite summit fresh with snow—
and above a sky-blue ceiling fresco.

IV To be there

I wanted to be there
at home with everyone and standing upright
mokopuna of his marvellous year
or shambling   speechless   tearful
bringing up the rear. I wanted to be there.

Each death is different. Every tangi wakes us.

I've had a few fathers since first questioning God the given—
he was the one found   chosen   taken   read aloud
more detached   observant   talkative   silent   specific   humane
hard-edged   able to compass and encompass   trenchant

& once I'd got to know him   always alert
reflective genial kind   careful not to hurt
at whose hands & feet I now lay flowers.

V 'Spectacular Blossom'

Mock up again summer, remembered crimson Christmas needles
for her whose feet slipped into shallows
as he lay on sand, propped on an elbow
a hand shading his eyes
the better to hold her spangled on the sea
before she swam into his mind
who now with every wave holds him
as the knees of light crash down.

—Niedernhausen, Germany, September 2001

Watching Eileen at a poet's wake

remembering Alan Brunton (1946–2002)

So still she sits
contained
as a Buddha, vase, caress
listening as her mother did at Mass—
her crammed coloured *kete* poised
& nearly spilling to the floor
forgotten things-to-do
books to read, crayons, pencils—

but she's too neat to knock it
is attentive only
to his words his friends read
his life continuous.

Does she realise
his romantic broil
his Übermensch on the swagger
his vermilion eye & mind & lip
his mask, his raunchy rhetoric
his kick-starts of register

need her
as an actor needs
a stage,
this audience.

Nikau at Punakaiki

i.m. Stewart Whaitiri 1956–2002

Warm north   cold south   salt mists   light falls
& nikau rocketing up out of the bush
in column clusters frilled and banded
for a queen—and eastwards inland   bush
more bush   in shrouded thicknesses of green
& rainbows   rainbows
the sky shot through with them.

West out to sea—these rocks
layered upon layer in thundering funnels
down to kelp   flinging & slapping
through the lacy sea that swells and slumps.

Your tipuna gave this land to all.
What wise blood ran in you.

Requiem at Torbay

i.m. George Wyllie McConnell 1934–2000
Canadian exploration geologist

The bay's pontoon
flung by the three day storm to the length of its chain
beached with the kelp a dog sea howled up.

Sea waves race in sluice out beyond the grassy bank & pines
& I know you're gone
'to the big gold mine in the sky'
old mad gorilla mate

I hope in your boots & jacket of pockets
carrying your pick—
you, who first showed me the world
in your palm—

I drank your kava.

You are gone—
flung out so hard by your own storm
you broke your chain
& kept on flying

no rock could hold you
no tor keep you hanging on
no island rescue
no safe yacht harbour.

Staunch

i.m Michael King 1945–2004 & Maria Jungowska 1949–2004

I'd have wished you a gentler death
in keeping with generosity & deft, liquid speech
yours of right, Michael, not this bizarre
fireballing out, though your friend said,
with your wit, you might have appreciated it.

I'll remember you both differently, Maria's
dark silk falling either side of her face, her cool
mind, German I, '67, University of Auckland—
her olive voice, Polish; & at Opoutere, her quiet
serving of our tea & a torte chock-full
with pecans, amidst the talk, the laughter.

And you, in tandem again after 22 years, on one of
the musical backseats of the *Words on Wheels* 2002
mini-bus, touring the Waikato—your transporting
us all into the Ur-realms of the rainbow god with
flaming hair, Uenuku in Te Awamutu, dredged
from Lake Ngaroto, Uenuku who guided a canoe
reincarnated as Tuwhata, become a sign of learning;

or our chuckling all the way back from Raglan
with tales of Frank, Janet, Karl, Bub, Keith, Pat
with a confidant's joy, cheek & reverence all at once;
or your charming the kids with story at your
sister's Southwell School when a national holiday
shut our tour down. Whose list stops?

You showed us ourselves. Helped us start to
differentiate our story. Stories.
Maori and Pakeha. Amassed infinite detail
perspective. For years and years.

Five months ago you told John Campbell
(who said you'd got a beautiful sparkle
in your eyes) you'd met everyone, written
everything, been everywhere you wanted—
knew life was a great gift, it had to be lived well

said you'd had a good crack at it; you'd
already had more than most, wished to see
grandchildren arrive, grow up—knew how
precious health is. Then took treatment
for ungentle cancer, survived it.

But who can staunch this?

You, in a dinghy happiest on a Coromandel inlet
fishing. How we all wish you this tall order, now.

Silence / speech

i.m. Michael King 1945–2004
i.m. Maria Jungowska 1949–2004

Silence is the real follower of death
the vivid emptiness—
where before a voice spoke
into a definite space & you heard it

it's inscribed now
on remembered sound
familiar as their handwriting
a person's face.

You realise they won't see a star again
or the lights of that plane
quite near the full moon
you just now thought was a star
coming clustered bright and unbelievably
straight towards you, soundlessly.

Once you see & hear the plane
you name it for them, as the day
names what the night holds.

We carry the dead
and we must now be
what the lives stood for.

Turning

i.m. Bridget McPhail 1960–2002

You think things before a death
you think somehow they'll survive
you're gunning for them   you're concentrating
each last centimetre of will with them

& then they say *let's get this show over soon*—
they're right & you can't wish it over quicker for them
& you can't wish it at all; then you see
it's the only way to go and by now you know

so many wobbly birds in flight   just taken off
that at least you can hope they'll do fingertip salutes
Hello! Hi! Oh, it's you. Where're you heading?
Yes, I knew him, knew her too

they're still living. And I'm winging my way . . .
The terns fly and fly—& it's all
a migration onto another beach, really.

love is a babe

a sequence of poems mostly around Beatrice's voice

Love is a babe . . .

I was a babe of eighteen when I fell—
twice Beatrice's age when Dante saw her.

I stood on a bridge between innocence
& knowledge—babes are like that—

nonchalant, petrified & full of love.
You looked up at the bridge, saw me,

stopped & I knew you knew in a sun flash
as Beatrice did. It chokes me still.

The world spins from under my hands.
Palms on my cheeks. I cannot hide.

I am six nines old. Beatus, it grows
& I carry it as Will said I would.

A portrait of Dante's younger self

'. . . such as he seems
In Giotto's fresco, holding up the flower,
Thinking of her whose hand, by Fate's strange plan,
He never touched on earth, but who, in dreams,
Oft led him into Heaven for an hour.'

From Dante's eyelid
falls a tiny triangle of folded white
she might have draped there
for him to hide
from seeing her again,
knowing too, she couldn't
protect him from himself—
knowing he saw nothing
but her eyes in his
whether or not he looked—
'her eyes being the source of love'.
Were he to remove
this token, hold it to his lips
then drop it for her to find—
she'd quickly lift it to her face
(should another see
from where it came)
& touch her lips with it,
'her mouth being the end of love'—
for 'the salutations of lovers
belong to acts of the mouth'.

Someone kissed me

Someone kissed me—
Is it blood or lipstick
on my cheek?

Was it a thought
brushed past me
or a moth's wing

but there, those crimson stains
on my skin, my white dress.
I walk the Lungarno

near the Ponte Sante Trinità.
He's evaporated
into the crowd

How shall I ever know him again
beyond this touch
and he so pure?

E la selva oscura, non cè?

He'd been to Ravenna
so I asked about the wood—
None! he laughed, then: *gone!*
solo la tomba di Dante

grave as a long low silent note—
la tomba la tomba
as if, as he'd fallen,
a great gong had rung out in Florence
and then stopped with a giant sob.

But it must once have been there
la selva oscura—the dark wood?
Yes, the one
we all take years
to come through—
yes, it existed.

Mercury

Is he god cold eyed or man
& these blue fires in his face?

Shall I touch to test, will my hand
go through him, angel unknowing

I'm alive or dead? But when I speak
he answers. My throat jams.

Does he too go numb after speech
or hope make real my ploy of him?

'The pure white diamond Dante brought to Beatrice'

I would give you everything   you must die to me
in life you are taken by life   I have no hold
I know I have place
for your friend once said   I'm there in your mind.

I should have loved you   to touch me
the one time you came to my bed
a green flash like the sun's   you there above me
I couldn't believe   when you'd gone.

A diamond is hard and is cold   however often
its facets light the blue flames of your face.
Wherever I look I must die to you   in life
I am taken by death   you have only this hold.

He reads his poem aloud

'Vide cor tuum—behold your heart'

He just keeps on saying
yes to me & making me his muse
& laughing with me as if
I were a sapphire found
on the grass & picked up
by one who names us
and throws us in the sea
so the water will shatter
& splinter on every beach
and the world will see us—
he, who ate my heart
I, who lie in his poem's.

Beatrice denies Dante her greeting . . .

'To what end do you love this lady of yours
since you cannot bear her presence?'

I deny him my greeting
for another sits between us
who the world sees as his—

(& though 'my secret is in truth
somewhat known to him',
the secret of my heart)

it is better for us both that this
other cares. So I let him think I'm
angry, who greeted her not me

& turn from him whose heart
I ate, for my time has come.
I wish him not to weep. I wish

that something is made new
through him, that which cannot
fail him—his words, his poetry.

Being Beatrice

Ultimately, being Beatrice
is all it's cracked up to be—
holiness demands much of her.

She must think
weigh things, decide
then let them go—

& she must always consider him—

whereas before
she stepped thoughtless
fearless & lightly as a muse.

Jousting

She's so glad she never said *never* to his
when are we going to have an affair? Instead
(knowing he wouldn't) she said *when you take*
the same emotional risk I would I will
and he whistled in even more admiration
but of the kind that (surprise!) showed
she'd outwitted him. She was so young then
she told his best mate who, after a consoling
drink, tried the same number (married too of course)
& wouldn't take Plato's way—*it's lovers or not, get it?*
haranguing her between St Helier's Bay fountain,
the Berkeley, Harris coffee shop & the seawall—
and try as she did to talk history, philosophy to
testosterone incarnate, he wouldn't give in—
so that was friendship forever exempted.
No wonder she went overseas. But men
here were like that then, except for Hermes
who ran along the waterfront, straight off
the sea—blond, sandals streaming—
he's the one held her till kingdom come
who never did, nor ever tried—
how she still favours him.

Meeting up with Dante down under

blue suits you she said noticing the radiant blue
of his parka lining his shirt & his eyes—wisely he

stayed neutral in reply, knowing theirs long since
though colourful, a relationship of innocence.

Beatus

There you are Beatus—
grey star on a dusky scarf
the moon halved by a cloud
& us sun-bathing in your palm
airy, toi-toi, blond feathers
staked like javelins
thrown to mark
a harbour—you are
the harbour & the yachts
in full light at full tilt—or

Orion, sword upside-down
spread-eagled on night blue—
you're the ninth step
of the ninth circle round
the tor, where a girl plaits
& waits for sight of your canoe,
paua eyes on the masthead gleaming
up from under as do those
of swordfish or marlin
or of a sea-god leaping.

notes

Many of these poems came because of my first attempts at reading Dante's *Commedia*, (known as The 'Divine' Comedy) and were sparked in particular by the last two stanzas of *Inferno* and what follows. In these lines Dante talks of himself and his companion, Virgil, coming out of the tunnel that leads from Hell into the 'hemisphere of water', located in the Antipodes, perpendicularly opposite Jerusalem and near the island-mountain of Purgatory. I've lightly followed Dante's pattern of addressing Calliope and then later several fellow poets in some of these poems, as all of them were written in the years after my return from Europe to again live in NZ in 1999, after twenty-five years away.

p.7 Section heading: dante's 'heaven'
* Alighieri Dante, *The Inferno of Dante,* Canto XXXIV, L 138–40, Robert Pinsky (trans).

p.10 Crux Australis—Te Paki o Autahi—Southern Cross
* Alighieri Dante, *Purgatorio,* Canto I, L 22–24:8, Robert M. Durling (trans).

p.11 Lily
The lily is the symbol of Florence, the city where Dante was born and from where he was exiled in 1302 at age 37.

p.12 Dante's 'heaven'
Of the three states of being or 'locations' Dante imagines in the three *cantiche* (parts) of the *Commedia, Purgatorio* most resembles the earth i.e. *Dante's 'heaven'*, as opposed to his 'heavenly paradise', *Paradiso.*

p.17 Sailing boats
origami—Japanese folded paper shapes.
wayang kulit—Javanese/Balinese shadow puppets.

p.19 Naked Ladies near Otama Beach, Coromandel Peninsula
(i) The line 'clear as god or glass' is from 'After the nit shampoo' in Anna Jackson's, *The Pastoral Kitchen.*
(ii) *Bang & Olufsen* are a Swedish electronics firm who produce top-quality loudspeakers.

p.29 Ming-blue fish
'Look, look well'—a well-known line from Dante.

p.49 Section heading *'Love is a babe'* *. . . a sequence of poems mostly around Beatrice's voice*
Dante was nine years old when he met Beatrice (Bica Portinari), who was in her ninth year. Both were later betrothed to and married other people, and she died in her twenty-fifth year around the time of Dante's birthday. Though never his wife or lover, she was his life-long muse and he writes of her in his youthful 'autobiography' *Vita nuova (New Life),* as well as in the *Commedia.*

p.50 'Love is a babe...'

The line is from William Shakespeare's Sonnet CXV.

p.51 A portrait of Dante's 'younger self'

(i) The initial quotation is from 'On the Fly-leaf of Dante's *Vita Nuova*'—*Eugene Lee-Hamilton.*

(ii) Lines in italics are based on those from: Alighieri Dante, *Vita nuova,* From her eyes . . .

(iii) Giotto di Bondone, *Paradiso,* detail of Dante Alighieri (1265–1321) c. 1336 (fresco) in the Museo Nazionale (Bargello) Florence, Italy. The folded handkerchief-shaped white missing piece of the fresco under Dante's eye was 'unhappily disfigured by a nail driven through the eye which was subsequently restored in the most arbitrary way'.

p.52 Someone kissed me

Dante first saw Beatrice near the Ponte Sante Trinità in Florence.

p.53 E la selva oscura, non c'e?

(i) And the dark wood doesn't exist any longer?

(ii) Dante died and was buried in Ravenna in 1321.

p.55 'The pure white diamond Dante brought to Beatrice'

(i) The title is from Eugene Lee-Hamilton's *What the sonnet is.*

(ii) 'a green flash'—a rare phenomenon, when the sun momentarily flashes green on the horizon.

p.56 He reads his poem aloud

Alighieri Dante, *Vita nuova,* 'and he so constrained her in his way that he made her eat this thing ablaze in his hand, which she consumed hesitatingly'; 3:5, Dino S. Cervigni & Edward Vasta (trans).

p.57 Beatrice denies Dante her greeting

This denial is 'one of Dante's six actual (and five fantastical, dream or mystical) "encounters" with Beatrice over a seventeen year period'. Lines in quotations based on those from: Alighieri Dante, *Vita nuova*—'to what end do you love . . .', Ibid, L 18:3; 'although your secret is in truth somewhat known to her . . .', Ibid, L 12:7.

p.61 Beatus

To reach Dante's earthly paradise and the Garden of Eden, you must climb the nine circles of Mt Purgatory to the top. I've imagined the tor as representing Mt Purgatory. A local Torbay myth has a young woman waiting for the return of her lover, as she sits on the tor watching the sea. The tor *is* difficult to climb, unless you are a child or very agile.

Designed, typeset, printed and bound
by John Denny at the Puriri Press
(email: dennyjhs@xtra.co.nz)
37 Margot Street, Epsom, Auckland 1003, NZ
in an edition of 200 copies.

Typeset in Centaur and printed on 104gsm
Starwhite natural text. Sewn and bound by hand.

Sources of images used:

Cover:	*Arthur Mee's Children's Encyclopedia,* London, Everybody's Publications Ltd, 1963.
p.9:	Google Images
p.25:	Adaption of a photo by Jan Kemp
p.37:	Google Images
p.49:	Google Images